T0124219

A Word to My Son

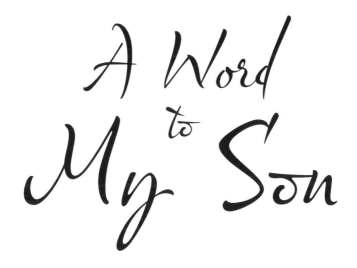

A Word to My Son

TIMELESS ADVICE FOR YOUNG AFRICAN
AMERICAN MEN AND WOMEN

JAY WILLIS

A WORD TO MY SON
TIMELESS ADVICE FOR YOUNG AFRICAN AMERICAN MEN AND WOMEN

iUniverse books may be ordered through booksellers or by contacting:

iUniverse
1663 Liberty Drive
Bloomington, IN 47403
www.iuniverse.com
1-800-Authors (1-800-288-4677)

ISBN: 978-1-5320-9455-2 (sc)
ISBN: 978-1-5320-9456-9 (e)

Library of Congress Control Number: 2020902322

Print information available on the last page.

iUniverse rev. date: 01/31/2020

CONTENTS

DEDICATION

To my son Martin: celebrating his third year of college.

ACKNOWLEDGMENTS

Thanks to my brother, Wade, for being one of the few decent role models I had as an isolated-rural youth. There weren't many possible role models, either in the family or in the community, but he served as a good family role model.

PREFACE

I write this book of sayings for my son, Martin. I figure he can relate to these sayings better than he could by having another lengthy book to read; since, he already has a lot of reading to do as a college student. I wanted to write a book of sayings specifically for him. I know his time is limited, and by giving him bite size chunks he might digest it better, much as a baby can best digest baby food.

I have always wanted both of my sons to attend college. My oldest son graduated several years ago, and is presently working in San Jose, California. I entitled this book, *Word to My Son: Timeless Advice for Young African American Men and Women*, because I wanted to celebrate my youngest son getting started on his third year of college.

My son doesn't like for me to preach to him, so I tried to devise a way to get the message to him. I have written whatever sayings I felt might help to motivate him. I hope he will digest these sayings and put them to good use. These statements contain information that my son, and I hope many other young people might find a practical use for them.

I put these together to try and give my son some directions. I realize that I didn't always communicate with him as he was growing up; and I understand that such attempts, after the fact, is no substitute for failed communications. I am attempting to pass this type of thinking on to my son and other young African American men and women; because, this type of critical thinking is badly needed in the Black community.

My brother moved from the Gulf Coast back to East Texas when I was twelve-years old. He served as my role model for several years until he moved back to the Gulf Coast. He taught me a lot while he was home; even though our contact was for only a few years. He didn't have much education, but taught me many practical aspects of life. My brother, Wade, was in many ways like a father to me. My father spent very little time at home. He worked 300 miles away and came home twice a month. We rarely talked. It is mind boggling to think of my own possibilities had I had a positive-consistent role model.

I have tried to serve as a role model for my sons in a similar way as my brother served for me; though, I may have sometimes missed the mark. I know the potential in such a situation. I realize that the Black community is lacking in adequate role models. By writing such a book of sayings, I can in some way be of some use to the Black community. By putting this book together, I'm trying to help prevent the strategic elimination of young Black men—especially (it is felt that young African American men are in greater danger of becoming extinct).

These sayings came mostly from my memory, my background, and my experiences, as well as my creative conscious. Some of them I have heard from others in my day to day existence—over a lifetime. They are mostly my own, but those that I memorized were modified, reconstituted, and rewritten to my taste. Some of the sayings from my memory are commonly used folk notions that it would be almost impossible to trace to their original source. It would take a lifetime of research to trace their origins. None of these sayings were deliberately taken from another source. The main point is being able to compile and share them with my son and other young African American men and women.

I avoided giving an explanation for each of these sayings because most of them seem self-explanatory. Most of them are also powerful but practical.

All of my other books may be previewed at {buybooks ontheweb.com}, {jaythomaswillis.com} or {amazon.com}.

ABOUT THE AUTHOR

JAY THOMAS WILLIS is a graduate of the University of Houston, Houston, Texas, where he earned a Masters' degree in social work; he is also a graduate of the Masters' degree counselling program at Texas Southern University, Houston, Texas. He attended undergraduate school at Stephen F. Austin State University, Nacogdoches, Texas, where he earned a B.S. degree in sociology and social and rehabilitative services.

He worked as a Clinical Social Worker for seventeen years, providing direct clinical services as well as supervision. He has been a consultant to a nursing home and a boys' group home; taught college courses in sociology, family, and social work in community college and university settings; and has worked as a family therapist for several agencies in the Chicago area. In addition, he was a consultant to a number of home-health care agencies in the south suburbs and Chicago. Mr. Willis is a past CHAMPUS peer reviewer for the American Psychological Association and the American Psychiatric Association. He also spent a number of years in private practice as a Licensed Clinical Social Worker in the State of Illinois.

Mr. Willis has traveled and lectured extensively on the condition of the African American community. He has written twenty-nine books, and written many journal articles on the subject of the African American community. He has written several magazine articles. He has also written Op-Ed Commentaries for the *Chicago Defender*, *Final Call*, *East Side Daily News* of Cleveland, and *Dallas Examiner*. He currently lives in Richton Park, Illinois with his wife and son.

ALSO BY JAY THOMAS WILLIS

Nonfiction

A Penny for Your Thoughts: Insights, Perceptions, and Reflections on the African American Condition

Implications for Effective Psychotherapy with African Americans

Freeing the African-American's Mind

God or Barbarian: The Myth of a Messiah Who Will Return to Liberate Us

Finding Your Own African-Centered Rhythm

When the Village Idiot Get Started

Nowhere to Run or Hide

Why Blacks Behave as They Do: The Conditioning Process from Generation to Generation

God, or Balance in the Universe

Fiction

As Soon as the Weather Breaks

Dream on: Persistent Themes in My Dreams

Hard Luck

Educated Misunderstanding

The Cotton is High

Poetry

Reflections on My Life: You're Gonna Carry That Weight a Long Time

CHAPTER 1

God and Spirituality

"God won't provide you
with things until you are
ready to handle them."

"We must all strive to not be more
religious but more like Christ."

"Black people need to
return to what is historical,
spiritual, and factual."

"Euro-centric biblical thinking
has done more to harm Black
people than any other system
of thinking on the planet."

"Jesus nor the devil has any
power except that which
we give each of them."

"Everybody has a point to make,
and they say whatever will
help them to make their point.
Ministers say whatever it takes to
get you to continue putting your
money in the collection plate."

"Religion has dissociated us from
our culture and our history."

"With respect to religion,
we depend on a lie to save
us from ourselves."

"God is always in control,
will deliver, and set you free;
because, he sees your heart."

"God will sometimes put
you to the test, to bring out

your true convictions, and
see what's in your heart."

"Get to know the God in you, and
there are no circumstances you
won't be able to overcome."

"When you have knowledge,
you don't need faith."

"When you have a relationship
with the Creator it empowers
you to make the necessary
changes in your life."

"Heaven is being in right-balance;
hell is being out of balance."

"There will be no rapture, and
Jesus is not coming back; no
one is going to be rescued."

"In regard to religion, we don't know history, we know biblical literature."

"We can't wait on a savior to take us out of the decadent situation we're in."

"We are the only people who can take a theology not based on fact and get joy out of it."

"The Almighty God uses ordinary people."

"The one true and Almighty God is not the God of biblical literature."

"The God of biblical literature is only a fabricated copy of the one true and living God."

"All things do work together
for the good as long as you
make a supreme effort."

"Every individual is anointed,
appointed, and has an assignment
from the Almighty God."

"God can cause anything
to happen, all you have to
do is believe, and make
a supreme effort."

"Your crisis is God's opportunity
to deliver a miracle."

"Don't believe God is; you
should know God is."

"We need to quit focusing
on dying and going to

Heaven and refocusing on living life to the fullest."

"God may forgive you, but you still may have to face the consequences for your negative actions."

"You may as well get out of the way of a blessed man; because, he'll run you through with his righteousness."

"The Almighty God exists in each of our lives."

"If your mind ain't right the power of God within you will become a destructive force."

"Heightening your spirituality
can increase your productivity."

"Don't put faith in things
that don't exist and
never have existed."

"God is a personal experience;
you can't simulate anyone
else's experience."

"Never depend on something
unreal to give you power in
your life on a daily basis."

"It's fallacious to depend on a
God concocted by other groups
to set you free and deliver you."

"Don't become so educated that you lose your appreciation for the Almighty God."

"God will give you grace for your season."

"Don't get distracted and forget to carry out your main God-given assignment."

"Any people who worship a god assigned to them by another nation are in trouble."

"Too much has gone into putting you asleep concerning religion to let you wake up."

"We are at the bottom of society; because, we have become disconnected from our spirituality."

CHAPTER 2

Knowing One's Limitations and Abilities

"Don't ever give up until you are completely exhausted and have no other options."

"Don't let anyone tell you that you can't be a success."

"You can make it if you try."

"The world is your canvass; paint on it whatever you will."

"Nobody can take your joy, and nobody can give you joy."

"You can never take away a man's education; though, you can take away many things from him."

"I did the best I could for my children as a result of my

level of conditioning. I know under different conditions I could have done better."

"Don't be afraid or have anxieties about anyone, for there is no one but the Almighty God superior to you."

"Don't be afraid to dream while keeping your dreams alive."

"You are the highest creation of God's imagination; no need to feel unworthy or inadequate."

"A man can be conditioned to accomplish almost any objective if the conditioning is severe enough."

"It is difficult to be productive when you live in filth, disease, and desperation."

"You cannot soar like an eagle hanging around with turkeys; a sense of power can come from those around you."

"It never hurts to let people know what your limitations are."

"Don't become helpless about your helplessness; you have power within yourself."

"Sometime things get difficult, but maintain your grip on what you know; the difficulties won't last forever."

"We Africans are at war
but fail to realize it."

"A dream ain't real, and
hope rarely ever comes."

"What brought you to
where you are can't take
you where you wanna go, if
it could you'd be there."

"There's no greater power,
other than God, than that
which already resides in you."

"Nobody can beat you being you;
you are a unique individual."

"How you see things is how you
have been taught to see them."

"We see the world not the way it is but based on how we've been conditioned to see it; it's hard to deliver us from our initial conditioning."

"Don't try to keep up with other people; because, other people don't have your assignment."

"Whatever you condition in a child it'll be there as an adult."

"Everybody has a right to their opinion."

"Nobody can do what you were born to do better than you."

"Unless you are God you will never know everything. All

you can do is present facts to the best of your ability."

"Everybody is not talented to the same degree; use what you have as if it counted."

"Many people are willing; few are able."

"Never overestimate yourself or underestimate others."

"In order to get where you are going you must know your destination."

"When you're at the bottom ain't no place to go but up."

"The truth shall set you free;
so, if you ain't free, you must
not know the truth."

"If you have no resources
you have no options."

"You can't get there if
you can't see it."

"No matter how old you are,
you're still here, and you've got
time to live your dreams."

"When some people are
dedicated to their ignorance
you have to leave them in it."

"Don't get so caught up in the
length of time that you forget
the value of time. It's not how

long you live, but what you
do with the time you have."

"You are unique and one of
a kind, it's good to have role
models, but be who the Almighty
God intended you to be."

"Focus on long-term, but also
focus on the here and now."

"Use your time and energy
to accomplish things that
are worthwhile."

"Discard those things that don't
add anything to your life."

"Be careful who you listen
to; don't be misled."

"Don't keep falling for the same okedoke, time, after time, after time...."

"If you keep trying something that doesn't work, try something different."

"Don't miss the mark of African consciousness by following the program of Euro-centric thought."

"Be careful not to wear out your welcome wherever you go."

"Don't get in the habit of not finishing what you started."

"When you put something out into the atmosphere that thing

will materialize, grow, and develop throughout the universe."

"It doesn't make sense to love your enemies or to turn the other cheek."

"Always be sure of your ground before you put your feet down."

"An unprepared mind will self-destruct."

"You can only operate from what you know."

"You can't get a new start until you come to an end."

"Identifying where you are equips you to find where you want to go."

"If you don't know who you
are you can't be yourself."

"To be stable you have
to know yourself."

"Be what you claim to be."

"Male energy without the
balance of female energy
is self-destructive."

"You must prioritize those
things in your life which will
aid in your development, and
remove those things that are a
hindrance to your development."

"Make tomorrow so big that
yesterday will be ashamed
to show its ugly head."

"When you get upset, most of the time the real issue is with you."

"Know what time it is in your life."

"You can have on several watches and still not know what time it is."

"Our greatest insecurity is in not knowing who we are."

"Don't put so much emphasis on tomorrow, for you can't get through to tomorrow, unless you get pass today."

"If something must end—it will."

"Obstacles in life are necessary; they prepare us for adversity."

"It's OK to feel down temporarily;
try a different approach when
you feel more positive."

"If you can't take care of your
responsibilities someone else will."

CHAPTER 3

Aggression

"Try to stay three steps ahead of others, because they will always try to push you back two steps, in that way you will always be one step ahead."

"When you begin writing your own story you'll start winning."

"If you fall off a horse get back on and keep riding."

"Don't let anyone block your progress."

"You must prepare now for your future."

"You must take responsibility for directing your life; no one else can do it for you."

"Haste makes waste."

"Keep trying; practice makes perfect."

"Relentless effort is the key to success."

"Don't wait for divine intervention; try to improve your circumstances with your own efforts."

"Don't let fear stop you from achieving your objectives."

"Take your time, but don't linger, you have plenty of time to get it right."

"Keep your eyes on the clouds,
your ear to the ground, and
your nose to the grindstone."

"Life is like a bicycle, you must
keep pedaling, or you will fall off."

"We should never be in the
business of conquering our own
people for the slave master."

"Good cannot triumph over
evil by retreating from it—
good must confront evil."

"Courage is just hanging in there
when you are scared to death."

"When we express ourselves,
it contributes to our growth."

"Quit putting off today for tomorrow, at some point you've got to realize, the time is right here—right now."

"Never give up; it's never too late."

"Make living your life your business."

"We must create a level of determination equal to that of racism."

"The only way to neutralize a conspiracy is to expose it."

"You must be proactive instead of reactive."

"We need to be aggressive in restoring an appreciation for African values within ourselves."

"You don't have to know everything; just know the important things."

"Never discount the unseen hand."

"A man has to get in the water to learn how to swim. You can't learn from a book, if you have never gotten in the water."

"You don't have to ask for forgiveness when you take control of your own behavior and action."

"You won't be happy until you come to grips with why you were placed on earth."

"Always be sure your priorities are in order."

"Everybody wants to be in control of their circumstances."

"You can get most of the things you want if you work hard enough, don't play games, and focus your energy."

"The truth is out there but you must go searching for it."

"Whatever you want to achieve in life, get started today."

"You can't improve if you don't make a concerted effort."

"Be sure you're on time and up to date: it's best to be early rather than late for all appointments."

"Use your imagination, it will take you to the deepest depths of your soul, and to far away places beyond."

"Think outside the box: use your creativity."

"If you fail to plan you plan to fail."

"If one attempt is not sufficient, try, try...again."

"If you work harder and smarter you will get results."

"Be a voice for those who can't speak; a light in the dark; and, an ear for the deaf."

"Fight for the poor, the downtrodden, and the disfranchised."

"Help those who are too weak to help themselves."

"When someone abandons you, all is not lost. Pick yourself up, dust yourself off, and get back in the game."

"We must learn how to let go, try a different solution,

seek guidance; don't continue
to frustrate yourself."

"Time will come when it
doesn't look like it will get
any better, but you must
stand on what you know."

"Don't get scared; get ready."

"Never allow other people's
negative energy to take
over your space."

"Don't wait on someone else
to answer the call; stand
up and be counted."

"Don't wait until tomorrow, do it
today, it must begin with you."

"If you are busy taking care of business you will have enemies."

"You are the only person who can reverse your oppression."

"For Black men, the game consists of indoctrination, emasculation, frustration, and termination."

"Black men should keep the warrior spirit, and don't be a sellout; it's time to stand up and be a soldier."

"Hope is nothing but a failure of individuals to aggressively pursue their objective."

"It's nice to listen to someone else's views, but find out the validity of these views for yourself."

CHAPTER 4

The Consequences of One's Behavior

"No one can succeed in life
without a well-thought-out plan."

"Take your time and
accomplish your objectives
one step at a time."

"Each time you make a mistake,
the next time try to get it better."

"Learn to profit from
someone else's mistakes
rather than your own."

"Putting your hands on
anyone inappropriately
is a major violation."

"A friendly word can create
much good will."

"You can lead a horse to water, but you can't make it drink."

"It's hard to love again once you've been badly hurt."

"Whatever is done in the dark will eventually come to the light."

"The person who seeks the truth will find it."

"The person who seeks a lie will find it."

"If you can't demonstrate what you say, you're just talking loud and saying nothing. You must be able to apply what you say."

"If you avoid adversity it
will only weaken you."

"Reading does for your mind
what brushing and flossing
does for your teeth, keep
it from deteriorating."

"Life is what you make it."

"If you look for something
negative long enough in your
situation you will probably find it
sooner or later. The same goes if
you look for something positive."

"You can only maintain a
notion of superiority at a
very high expense."

"Don't give people the benefit of the doubt at your expense."

"Indecision is more destructive than no decision."

"Don't let fear stop you from doing what you are capable of."

"Vulnerability is not always a sign of weakness; in order to grow it is necessary to be vulnerable. People don't like to be vulnerable because they fear failure."

"Fear will keep you from making progress."

"I will stand on everything I know today even though I may have to change it tomorrow."

"The worst thing you can do
to a bird is to clip its wings."

"It's so good, loving somebody,
when somebody loves you back."

"Too many of us do the right thing
at the wrong time; therefore,
we miss our appointed time."

"Going through adversity
helps us to grow."

"In order to dream you've
got to stay asleep."

"One's ability to smile
should not be connected to
currency in his pocket."

"You can't hold a man down in the gutter without getting some dirt and grime on yourself."

"Fear is a matter of choice."

"Sometimes you have to think yourself happy; don't let others make you feel bad about yourself."

"If you don't use it you lose it."

"Spending too much time with the distractions of others will distract you as well."

"Intellectual masturbation leads to egotistical ejaculation."

"When we stand up the whole game is over."

"When we don't listen, we deserve the consequences of our dedicated ignorance."

"If you've never been in the valley you can't appreciate the mountain top."

"At some point you've got to forget about if I would have just, if I could have just, or I should have just. Make a decision and follow it through."

"You must realize when you reach the point of no return."

"What you're doing does not matter as much as what you're learning from doing it."

"Struggle tempers us for the difficulties in our lives."

"If you study too long you will often study wrong."

"Be sure your left hand knows what the right one is doing."

"It's no wonder some people have abnormal problems in their lives. They create them by the way they live."

"Wait until you see the white of their eyes before you speak. We no longer live in slavery; it's okay to look a man in his eyes. If you don't look a man in his eyes when you talk to him, you are seen as suspect."

"When you consider negotiating, remember to bring something to the table."

"When you get afraid, consider how wonderfully you are made."

"You will be held accountable for the words that you speak. They will either justify you or condemn you."

"Try not to go around in circles, ending up where you started."

"Don't tell another person something to live by if it doesn't work for you."

"As a result of not knowing
the truth you must pay
the consequences."

"Wrong thinking is the seed that
leads to a harvest of failure."

"How you think will determine
the direction of your life."

"What you don't know
can hurt you."

"Forget the things behind
you and reach forward."

"When you plant a seed, the
fruit is much more productive."

"Every situation is an opportunity
to make a difference."

"Be a builder instead
of a destroyer."

"Revenge is best served cold."

"Be careful what you wish
for you just might get it."

"Fulfillment in life comes with
living out your creative purpose."

"When you're an animal, and you
constantly go after something for
dinner that is faster than you are,
you're going to always be hungry."

"Our redemption depends on us
getting in touch with our history."

"Don't allow other people's idiosyncrasies to control your emotions."

"You can't get better as long as you are bitter."

"We become most passionate about what we can't validate."

"If you bring truth to power, power will have to come to truth."

"If you don't know who you are you can't empower or define yourself."

"Your deliverance depends upon your own personal sense of empowerment."

"Don't put a log on a fire that
you wish would burn out."

"If you go through what it takes
to become a wizard, by the very
nature of becoming, you might
end up a punk in the process."

"Never let anyone play pendulum
with your feelings; once you
decide to let it go—let it go."

"No matter how painful, take
every experience as a learning
experience, don't hold on."

"No one is perfect, and we
will make mistakes."

"It takes as long to heal as
it does to get ourselves in
difficult situations."

"Something you desperately need
can be obtained from someone or
some activity you don't enjoy."

"When you get tired, hold
on, help is on the way."

"Don't live your life in a negative
way; expect something
positive to happen."

"You're not a failure until you
absolutely quit and give up."

"Don't focus on your enemy;
keep your eyes on the prize."

"If you fall in a hole, and there's a shovel in the hole, don't start digging trying to escape."

"If you listen to what your enemies say about you, sometimes you'll begin to doubt yourself."

"You are where you are today, in part, because of decisions you made yesterday."

CHAPTER 5

Change and Action

"He who laughs first doesn't always get the last laugh."

"In order to be successful in this life, you must at some point remove the veil of ignorance."

"Always let people know where you stand and where they stand with you."

"You can't ride both sides of the fence."

"Things may look bad now, but get a goodnight's sleep, and they will look better in the morning."

"Kind and gentle people sometimes talk loud, because they

have been badly hurt, and want to keep others at a distance."

"Don't sit there and whine about the situation; get up and do something to solve the problem."

"Do something other than fight, find fault, and disagree with your brother."

"Black people must come into proper consciousness and redefine themselves."

"Black people cannot reconstruct themselves as long as they're using a Euro-centric paradigm."

"Anything worth doing should be done as soon as possible."

"Falsehoods are like dandelions, hard to root out."

"Don't become arrogant because you have acquired some information."

"The educated must become a voice in the wilderness for change."

"No use closing the barn door: it is too late for most of us; the door has already been left open, and the horse is out to pasture."

"We need to get serious about our commitment to change."

"The first thing we must do
to bring about change is to
properly educate ourselves."

"Everyone has the power and
the ability to do what's right."

"Don't be uncomfortable
with change; change is
the only constant."

"Life is for the living, so live it."

"It's best to make changes
in your life gradually."

"If you want to get better, hang
with people at a higher level."

"Life is like a pendulum: it
swings back and forth; it
has highs and lows."

"You only pass this way once;
try and make it a better place."

"Plan your actions, you
will surprise even yourself
with your success."

"Power is the ability to achieve
goals. The biggest barriers to
achieving goals are powerlessness,
negativity, and helplessness."

"Common sense is not
so common: get all the
education you can."

"Take a good look at yourself
and make that change."

"Doing it right the first time
applies to any endeavor
you embark upon."

"Be convincing that you will not
give up and you will not quit."

"Whatever you do, make it
the best job you can. Even if
you sweep floors for a living,
be the best floor sweeper
there has ever been."

"A pig wearing lipstick
is still just a pig."

"Be a light that sits on a hill and illuminates the way rather than be the consuming darkness."

"Be sure you know who needs to make the adjustment you or the other person."

"You will never here the powers-that-be talk about a savior coming to save them from their decadent plight."

"Always express an attitude of gratitude."

"We have lost our history, and have forgotten who we really are."

"Don't try to raise a man up who wants to stay down."

"We are living in a time when, if you don't employ yourself, you might be out of business."

"We are confused enough without adding to that confusion with alcohol and drugs."

"Don't allow anyone to cause you to be mainly self-absorbed, self-promoting, conceded, or irreverent."

"We must maintain a positive–cultural view of ourselves."

"Surgery is often painful but necessary for healing."

"Ask a dead rabbit if there's any power in his rabbit's foot."

"When most people come
into your life, they know
one day they will leave. Love
people when they come, and
love them when they go."

"Don't become consumed with
the paralysis of analysis."

"Don't kill the messenger because
you don't like the message."

"Always take it day by day, and
on Sundays—hour by hour."

"Today is the first day of
the rest of your life."

"Everything created solves
a problem; what problem
will you solve?"

"The situation dictates your actions."

"Move on but remember the past."

"You must reclaim your African story."

"It's time for a revolution in our minds."

"When you know you need to make a change, and you don't make it, then you deserve whatever negative consequences you get."

"When you control a man's thinking you don't have to worry about his actions."

"When you tell one lie
you've got to keep telling
lies to be consistent."

"What goes around
comes around."

"Be careful how you treat
people on your way up; you
might meet these same
people on your way down."

"A good and thoughtful man
is never violent unless it's
completely necessary."

"Sometimes it's better to keep
negative thoughts to yourself."

"Do more loving and a
lot less judging."

"It's important to
keep your focus."

"The most difficult thing
for some is thinking."

"Life consists of a series
of ups and downs."

"Activity without accomplishment
is an exercise in futility."

"You will either change or
become a victim of change."

"Never try to operate from
someone else's paradigm."

"Keep your present position,
or do what it takes to get
where you want to go."

"Don't pass it on: stop teaching the lies you were taught."

"Don't keep looking back when life has moved you on."

"Don't get trapped in your own illusion of temporary satisfaction and forget that you need to move forward."

"The power of the truth will awaken Black people."

CHAPTER 6

Destructiveness

"Violence is not appropriate in most circumstances; though, it is easy to resort to violence."

"One of the most effective ways to destroy a people is to put in place a program that will destroy their identity, culture, and spirituality."

"Some people are too low to get even with."

"People who are trying to kill you don't care how you die."

"If a man is trying to kill you don't worry about making him angry."

"You can carry a lie for a long time, but it won't last forever."

"Most people are a
tough nut to crack."

"Don't be guilty of
perpetuating ignorance."

"Don't refuse to give up
on something that has
proven over and over that
it's not going to work."

"No drug is more powerful
than your mind."

"Once they branded us with their
branding irons; now we spend our
hard-earned money to buy their
clothing brands voluntarily."

"When you don't criticize and analyze you create the conditions for your own demise."

"Even a rat has more than one hole to hide in."

"Anyone can be critical; be sparing in your criticism."

"If there's a hell below we're all gonna go."

"An African mind encased in European philosophical thought is self-destructive."

CHAPTER 7

Money

"Put your money where your mouth is; because, talk is cheap."

"You won't enjoy prosperity until you can appreciate life without it."

"Live for meaning and purpose rather than money."

"In order to prosper you must have a respect for money."

CHAPTER 8

Self-Preservation

"To uproot a people from
a lie and plant in the soil of
truth might kill them."

"Don't listen to anyone
who doesn't have your
best interest in mind."

"Master your strengths, and
fortify your weaknesses, if they
are relevant to your success."

"Be down for however
long it takes to accomplish
your objective."

"We must not allow ourselves any
identification other than African."

"Some people are good at impression management but are weak and ineffective otherwise."

"Always try to exercise good judgment."

"If someone is trying to take you away from your purpose you must get away from them."

CHAPTER 9

Self-Hate

"A person who is dissatisfied
with himself will spread
dissatisfaction to his friends."

"We must learn to appreciate
ourselves; we have an appreciation
for everybody but ourselves."

"We have gotten comfortable
with being on the bottom of the
social ladder of accomplishment."

"Some people are like gravity:
their natural inclination
is to pull you down."

CHAPTER 10

On Liberation

"We are at war for the liberation and empowerment of the Black mind."

"We must learn that we are all one, and must learn to move and be as one."

"You must learn the necessity of your own sense of empowerment."

"Black people need more leaders who can speak to them in a way to wake up the blind, deaf, and dumb."

"We are all beautiful, terrible, ugly, clean, nasty, ridiculous, gracious, mean, kind, respectful, considerate, limited, powerful, weak, alienated, estranged, angry, hopeful, delightful, determined, dejected, detested...."

"Make your words those of healing and direction rather than destruction."

"There is no excuse for ignorance. Everything you need to know can be found in a library."

"In order to make progress in your life, you must eradicate the categorical lies about yourself."

"Your deliverance depends on your personal sense of empowerment."

"At all times think about
your healing, development,
and empowerment."

"Don't depend on a fabricated
sense of history to give
you a sense of power."

"We must break the last
bond of slavery: the slave
master's religion."

"Don't be a victim of selective
biblical attention."

"Before you can set yourself free
you must realize you're a slave."

"Each one, teach one;
each one, reach one; and,
each one, save one."

"Along with your cultural awareness you need spiritual power to liberate yourself."

"Growth requires an admittance of ignorance."

"In order to be liberated; you must stay in faith, stay in focus, and stay connected."

"The system we live in was not designed to bring about our liberation."

"We need institutions of liberation in our community."

"The words that you believe will either liberate you or

forever enslave your mind. Be careful what you believe."

"A sense of a future would help to improve the conditions of the Black community."

"No permanent sense of empowerment can take place without properly educating of young people, while giving them a sense of consciousness."

"We must all remain vigilant because of the warfare over the empowerment of the Black mind."

"No oppressor in the history of this or any other country has taught the oppressed how to overcome their oppression. We will have to liberate ourselves."

"We must develop unity and healing in our community, or we are headed for severe self- and other-destruction."

"We must return to the true African center of ourselves."

"You must create your own job and quit looking for other groups to give you one."

"In order to liberate yourself you must learn to think for yourself."

"Some of us are more of a slave now than when we were in the fields picking cotton."

"The most important thing in a person's life is what he believes. The way to control a person is to control what he believes."

"Be sure you get an education from your schooling as opposed to training: an education teaches you how to think rather than what to think, training only teaches us what to think."

"It's time for our resurrection, liberation, and empowerment."

"We must bring those back to life who have been anesthetized."

"Free yourself so that you can free others."

"The only thing that will free your African mind is to understand the system which has oppressed you."

"Meaningless and empty words, without power, fade like snow in a frying pan."

CHAPTER 11

Honor and Respect

"Rescue and reach a person with compassion, love, and tact, don't attack them."

"Respect, courtesy, and understanding will never go out of style."

"At all times have respect for your fellow man."

"As a country we can't treat people unjustly, while continuing to espouse liberty, justice, and equality, something has to give."

"Even a dog gets tired of being mistreated."

"If you treat people with dignity, respect, and kindness, most of them will treat you the same."

"Respect yourself and others will wonder who you are; despise yourself and others will wonder what you are."

"A man doesn't have to be worth much to be worth something to somebody."

"If you receive aid and comfort from people, you should dispense that same comfort to others. Share your comfort zone."

"We must not forget our historical greatness and work to become great once again."

"People believe something is wrong or right based on what they've been taught."

CHAPTER 12

Assessing Your Situation

"You cannot define yourself
by those who do not wish
for you to succeed."

"We live in an awesome world.
Make it an awesome period in your
life. Peace to you; may God bless
you. Live simply. Love generously.
Care deeply. Speak kindly."

"Don't be preoccupied with the
end of the world; live your life as
if there is no end to your time."

"There are many lies perpetrated
in society, you must figure out
the truth, and decide what you
are going to do about them."

"You can never remove all
flaws from your life, but you

can continue to work on improving these flaws."

"Don't speak like a peasant: it's important that you speak the King's English."

"A young person will only make the trek to adulthood once; learn all you can along the way."

"Do the best you can to get life as correct as possible, so when you get older you won't have to wish you could have gotten it better."

"It's better to have an education and not need one, than to need an education and not have one."

"You will never forget your
high school and college days;
make the best of them,
both socially, academically,
and psychologically."

"If children had better teachers
in childhood and adolescence,
they could avoid a lot of
unnecessary anxiety and fear."

"Nothing is ever as good or
bad as we think it is."

"Most people have similar
fears, shed similar tears, and
die in so many years."

"It takes good families, good
schools, decent churches, and

decent communities to produce healthy-functional individuals."

"My parents did the best they could with what they had; I did the best I could with what I had; and, I hope you can do better with what you have. Just try not to pass on any negativity."

"When your heart is right, and you treat people right, you have nothing to fear."

"When you don't know who you are, you search for an identity that will give you validity."

"When you have to go to the literature, that you

didn't write, to give you an identity, you're in trouble."

"Sometimes we need to believe certain things because we don't know what else to believe."

"It would be better to die than to refrain from doing things because you are fearful about the consequences."

"It's great to have the ability to make choices, but it's even greater to be chosen."

"This is what life is, and that's all it's gonna' be."

"It's a frustrating experience when things in reality are other than what they are supposed to be."

"The Almighty God has chosen us, our ancestors are guiding us, and our children are counting on us."

"In any situation, be sure you have all the information before you make an important decision."

"Understand the game before you become the game."

"Don't let anyone convince you that your game is lame. That they're together and you're not. We all have areas of weakness."

"If you don't understand the game, you are the game."

"Don't let them directly influence you, but the powers-that-be set their daily traps, waiting on you to make a mistake, so they can put you away."

"You have a most wonderful call on your life. You owe it to the Creator to find out what it is. Don't hide your talents."

"What looks like a put back is a put up for your come back."

"A man can knock you down but can't keep you down; whether or not you stay down is your responsibility."

"People are not that different.
Inside we are all people afraid
of dying or getting hurt."

"Your crisis is the wind that
God is throwing to you
to take you higher."

"You may not be overly happy,
but this is the best life you have;
do the best you can with it."

"You don't have to accept
anything you don't
want to accept."

"A map is meaningless if you don't
know where you are on the map."

"When your mind and emotions
are distorted you become
a beautiful monster."

"It will be necessary to stay where
you are or make that change."

"Before you go around the
world looking for treasures,
check the inventory in
your own warehouse."

"If it sounds impossible
it probably is."

"Be more concerned with the
log in your eye than the splinter
in your brother's eye."

"Other than your family, no one
else has to live with you but you,

so be sure to live your life in such a way as to please yourself."

"What you know is not all there is to know."

"You must have the right map to get you where you want to go. Sometimes it's the map rather than your attitude or behavior that keeps you from getting where you want to go."

"Don't fall into the trap of thinking, the way you see things is the way they are, or the way they should be."

"Sometimes what we see depends on what we want to see; it depends on our perspective.

Two people can see the same thing in two different ways, and both are right. The right principles don't change."

"Dependence on another person ends when you learn what they know."

"The ones who make policy designed the system for your dependency on it."

"If you don't know what you will be doing ten years from now, how're you going to plot a path for accomplishing your objectives?"

"Everything you've ever wanted is already in your life, merely awaiting your recognition of it."

"The most important thing you will ever do is to recognize your assignment on this earth."

"We have come a long way but have a lot more work to do."

"Destine for greatness, you are prepared for whatever you encounter, you just don't realize it yet."

"You were born for this moment, place, and time."

"Never forget where you came from."

"We are still as a people picking cotton and sharecropping."

"Without resistance in our lives
none of us would get very far."

"It's the abnormal people who
accomplish extraordinary things
in the world; normal people
just do what is expected."

"When your enslaver and
your oppressor look like your
Savior, you're in trouble."

"If a person can do no better than
his parents there has been no
inter-generational progress."

"There's no greater fulfillment
than to realize what you
were born for, so that you
and others can live."

"Things are not always as they seem. Just because a person frowns at you doesn't mean he hates you. Because he smiles at you doesn't mean he likes you. People have various facial expressions for many different reasons."

"The truth is not something you believe; it's something consistent with fact and reality."

"It's easy to see what's apparent, but you need to see what's hidden between the lines."

"Don't be a slave to culture; have a mind of your own."

"It's no failure to have great goals and not achieve them. The failure is when you have no goals at all."

"You are what you are today because of the choices you made yesterday."

"Take one call at a time, and quit being obsessed with the call on the other line."

"Go out and get involved; don't just sit around and be inactive."

"Don't worry about what you can't do; focus on what you can do."

"Stay humble and stay hungry."

"You must learn to be comfortable being uncomfortable."

"Fear does not stop tomorrow's sorrows; it only weakens today's strengths."

"He who has light should not base his life on the darkness of the world."

"Truth is useless if you don't know the truth for yourself."

"Define yourself; don't allow circumstances to define you."

"Give something back to those who made a way for you; don't just take, and take, and take...."

"The difficulties you go through
today may be setting you up
for a better tomorrow."

"Let go of yesterday's mistakes,
and press on toward your future."

"What seems like a bad situation
might lead to a great revelation."

"The truth hurts when all
you know is the lie."

"Desperate situations call
for desperate measures."

CHAPTER 13

On Authority

"People who do not have a sense of personal power feel bitter, resentful, and confused."

"The powers-that-be has already assigned you a position in life; you must resist falling into this position."

"Because you don't have power over a negative situation today doesn't mean you won't gain the necessary power a year from now. Keep working at it."

"The powers-that-be usually will inform you of their intent only after it is too late for you to do anything about it."

CHAPTER 14

Making Friends

"At a young age friends are won and lost in a brief span of time."

"Only trust some people as far as you can throw them."

"Everybody who calls you a friend may not be your true friend."

"Your success depends not on how others define you, but on how you define yourself."

"We are the way we are because of the way we think about ourselves."

"Be careful in choosing your friends; you never know what burdens others are walking around with."

"Nobody is going to like
everything about you."

"The more knowledge you gain,
you might find yourself with
fewer and fewer friends."

"Try to always be around
positive people; negative people
will make you negative."

"If you give off negative
vibes you will get negative
vibes given back to you."

"Never turn your back
on a true friend."

"Don't let even your friends keep
you from your ambitions."

"Everyone is not going to like you, and you are not going to like everybody."

"Young people fall in and out of love like trout playing in an open stream beneath the sun and shadows."

"Young people fall in love with anything young, warm, and beautiful."

CHAPTER 15

Understanding

"Learning occurs a little at a time."

"Anything broken down into
its simplest components
can be understood by the
average individual."

"Be wise and humble enough to
at least consider what others say;
even if they don't agree with you."

"Understand when it is
unrealistic to expect certain
results from certain people."

"Don't let anything blind
you to your personal and
psychological power."

"In all your getting, get
an understanding."

"Evaluate carefully what
people tell you."

"Understanding is the best
thing you can have."

"Not everyone will make it to the
promised land. Liberation is for
all, but not all is for liberation."

"Warmth and understanding
always give new life."

"For every season there is a
purpose; it is important to know
and understand the times."

"Take advantage of,
don't waste time."

"You can only possess
time for a season."

"It's not necessary to always
understand, but we must
always have trust."

"It's not the actual situation
that determines how we see
things, but it's our individual
perception of the situation."

CHAPTER 16

On Reality

"I realize you are saved,
but saved from what."

"You can't make yourself
better until you admit the
reality of your situation."

"You're not admitting defeat
when you admit to your reality."

"We must wake up to the reality
behind the appearance."

"If you're weak accept that
reality, but in the meantime
try to build your strength."

"If you wake up every morning,
that's the only miracle
you're likely to witness."

"Make-believe is only
healthy in children."

"Don't place expectations
on people that you have no
right to place on them."

"Don't lose your perspective
on life; always know
where you're at."

"If one person says something
negative about you, maybe you
should consider whether it's
true, but if a lot of people are
saying it, it probably is true."

"Be careful about making
promises you know
you can't keep."

"It's time for Black people
of the world to wake up and
unite; look around you."

"Always remember who you are
and what your assignment is."

"You must always pay
attention to your intuition."

"Don't be taken in by outward
appearances; look toward
the person's inner nature."

"Be careful what you
accept as real."

"We must learn to see the reality
behind the appearance."

CHAPTER 17

Personal Issues

"Never let it be said that your mother and father raised a fool."

"Never let it be said that your mother and father raised a quitter."

"Keep your head toward the sky."

"Keep thinking positive."

"The only way to reach a person is to relate to them on their level."

"No one can go through life and keep it all together—at all times."

"We make a big mistake when we take for granted that other people have it all together, and we don't have anything together."

"No matter how bad you feel about life, always take the good with the bad, and the bitter with the sweet."

"Anxiety and fear are usually unnecessary; take it as it comes and do your best to deal with it as effectively as you can."

"Keep your thoughts pure and your mind on the greater good."

"No matter what the circumstances, don't let anyone talk you into doing something against your better judgment."

"Take every opportunity to create another opportunity for yourself."

"We are all on a journey of discovery of ourselves; we are blessed if we ever find out who we really are."

"Sometimes we get too hung up on the way things appear to be. Learn to listen to your inner voice. Frequently things aren't what they appear to be."

"Everyone must learn to manage his emotions."

"Be yourself; you should have nothing to hide."

"You must rid yourself of things that are no longer useful in your life."

"Once you know yourself, you'll know what you need to do for yourself."

"It's not what people think of you, but what you think of yourself that matters."

"Before you criticize anyone else, be sure you take a good long look at the man in the mirror."

"Conflict can be good, but if you find yourself in constant conflict with a person, you should put some distance between the person and yourself."

"Our needs can sometimes overpower our rationality."

"Before looking down on someone else, walk a mile in their shoes."

"Don't spend your life trying to make people happy who don't want to be made happy."

"Be sure you care about things that matter and have the right priorities."

"Keep a right head and a right heart."

"How we get started in life is not nearly as important as how we finish."

"What you do can sometimes speak so loudly that it's hard to hear what you say."

"You're not in proper
balance until your reason
controls your emotions."

"The person who conquers his
thoughts cannot be conquered."

"When you think right
all else will be right."

"Be the person you were
created to be."

"Most people have a lot of
junk in their trunks."

"In the process of living you collect
a lot of junk in your trunk."

"People don't let go of
their junk easily."

"People want what you've
got, but they don't want
to be where you were."

"Stand on the solid ground
of personal discipline."

"Don't let anyone bring negative
energy into your space."

"You must face up to
your shortcomings"

"Practice continuous
self-examination."

"Recognize your personal union
with God the Almighty."

"If you listen to your enemies long enough you will start believing them yourself."

"You must get rid of small-time thinking."

"Don't let tragedy have to come to make you realize what's important in life."

"We have been stripped of our identity, and redirected to the identity of those that initiated the cause of our destruction."

"We are so devoid of an identity that we must look into literature of our oppressor to find an identity."

"Don't let your flaws and
faults overtake you."

"We must work to heal
ourselves and each other."

"It's most difficult when you fall
and have no one to support you."

"We all need each other for
our mutual survival."

"Believe only in what you have
found to be the truth for yourself."

"As long as you live by someone
else's paradigm you will never
be a complete individual."

"If you carry negative
energy, you're going to
be negative energy."

"If you wallow in your tragedy you
will multiply the effects of it."

"How you see the world
has everything to do with
how you function in it."

"If you want your life to be
better you must work on
your inner self first; you must
work from the inside out."

"You are responsible for your own
happiness; no one has control
over your happiness but you."

"Find security in yourself, not in forces outside yourself; when you are principle-centered, all of life experiences and opportunities are chances to gain knowledge."

"Freedom comes with knowledge, and knowledge brings power."

"If you ignore your inward thoughts long enough, when they do speak, you won't hear them."

"Your decisions in life should be based upon what you can live with."

"What you see depends on from what position you are looking."

"Examine your subliminal programming, because in many ways it controls your behavior."

"Some people avoid the truth; some people seek it."

"Peace, happiness, and love are three elements in a healthy existence; you must have these three things before you can share them with others."

"We must learn to be human; it does not come naturally."

"If you don't know how you got into difficulties yesterday, you will likely get into more difficulties today."

"If you don't determine your own destiny someone else will determine it for you."

"Sometimes you have to love people back to health, whether psychological or physical."

"I firmly believe that we should spend more time listening and less time talking, but keep your communication skills sharp."

"Question everything in your mind, and use your imagination to the fullest."

"Sacrifice for many things, but never sacrifice your health, whether physical or psychological."

"If people talk about you, be careful what you pay attention to; it doesn't matter what people call you, but what you answer to."

"It's hard to define what normal is, but try to remain true to yourself."

"Don't be proud, haughty, and arrogant; but know and exercise your capabilities."

"Learn to take control of your behavior early in life; don't wait until you are about to close your eyes before you wake up."

"Don't let anyone tell you what is best for you."

"Let your heart lead the
way in all matters."

"Always be kind and respectful."

"Be the best at whatever you do."

"Don't let your past
determine your future."

"Without education, and hope
for a future, we are lost."

"Take hold and plan
for your future."

"Run the race before you; don't
run somebody else's race."

"How you see your predicament
is your predicament."

"Don't let anyone impose their negative reality on you."

"Learn to navigate through other systems so that you may feel empowered enough to master your own; don't let other systems consume you."

"If you haven't put anything into the pot, don't walk around with your hands held out."

"Paradise is different for everyone. If you ever find yours you will recognize it. When you find it, hold on, and don't let go."

"Listen to what people don't say as well as what they say."

"All you touch you change, and all you change will change you."

"Everybody doesn't have the same needs, but most of us need a purpose in life."

"So, you think nobody likes you; well, nobody probably thinks about you one way or the other; you barely even think about yourself."

"When you're called of God you don't have the option or the luxury of giving up."

"If you need drugs or alcohol to carry out any given activity, you need to cease engaging in that activity."

CHAPTER 18

Family

"Very few parents intend to harm their children. If they do so, they do it out of ignorance."

"I assumed my parents were ignorant, but the older I got, the smarter my parents got."

"Remember, people who come after you are counting on you."

"At times you will feel ashamed of your parents, and at times your parents will feel ashamed of you, but there is no reason for either."

"Parents do what they're conditioned to do, and children do what they're conditioned to do, no reason to place blame on either."

"Children do what you do
and not what you say do."

"When parents are in conflict
it sets the stage for their
child's destruction."

"Respect begins with
home and family."

"It's hard to accept negativity
from relatives; though, they
can frequently be as cold as
anyone on the street."

"Keep the home-fires burning!"

"We can't depend on society
to develop our children;
we must train and educate
them ourselves."

"Parents should set themselves apart from anything that won't allow them to be the most effective parents possible."

"A role model must be realistic for one to identify with and move in that direction."

"Always take care of home and family first."

Printed in the United States
By Bookmasters